Climate Strike

Written by Isabel Thomas

Contents

Collins

Listen to us!

In September 2019, millions of young people missed school to join **climate** strikes around the world. Holding signs and banners, they gathered in huge crowds outside government buildings in over 180 countries.

These children all demanded the same thing: that adults start to tackle the **climate emergency**.

It was the biggest ever climate protest and it came at the end of an incredible year, when children took the lead in speaking up for the environment. This is the story of how the school strikes for climate began and spread around the world, inspiring a generation of children to fight for the future of the planet.

JUST BECAUSE WE HAVE A SMALLER CARBON FOOTPRINT, DOESN'T MEAN WE CAN'T MAKE AN IMPACT!

The first climate strikes

For most Swedish children, Friday 20th August 2018 was the first day of a new school year. But in one classroom, 15-year-old Greta Thunberg's seat was empty. Instead, Greta was sitting on the cobbled pavement outside the Swedish parliament.

Greta's sign reads, *"School strike for the climate"*.

Ever since she was a young child, Greta had been alarmed by news about the harm humans were doing to the environment.

Fifth warmest January on record

Levels of greenhouse gases reach new peaks

EXTREME WEATHER CLAIMS LIVES AND DESTROYS LIVELIHOODS

Arctic heatwave melts sea ice

Where have all our insects gone?

She was frustrated that politicians didn't seem to be listening and weren't doing everything they could to tackle the emergency.

The Swedish **general election** was coming up. Greta decided she would miss school every day until the election to protest about the lack of action on climate change.

As well as her sign, she made leaflets explaining why she was breaking Swedish law by missing school.

I'm too young to vote. But Swedish law requires that I go to school. So I do this to make my voice heard and attract media attention to the climate crisis.

Greta was soon joined by other students, as well as some teachers and parents. The protest quickly attracted the attention of media around the world.

Fridays for Future

After the election, Greta returned to school for most of the week. However, she continued to strike every Friday and invited other young people to do the same. The word spread on social media.

By November 2018, around 17,000 students in 24 countries had joined in, missing school to demand action on climate change. Fridays for Future became headline news around the world.

People in power began to take notice. Greta was even invited to speak at the annual United Nations Climate Change Conference in December 2018.

You are never too small

In a calm voice, Greta stood up in front of thousands of politicians, climate leaders, scientists and business people and spoke on behalf of young activists around the world.

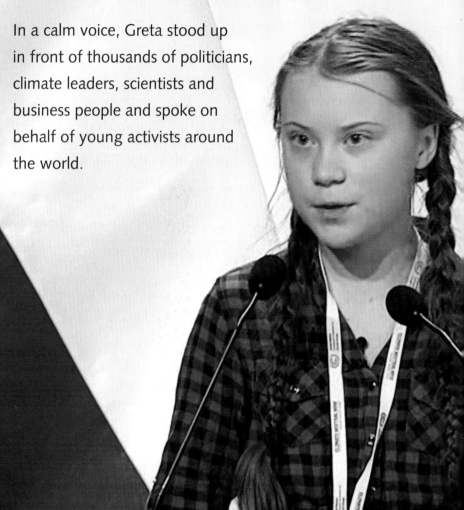

COP24·KATOWI

UNITED NATIONS CLIMATE CHANGE CONFE

POLAND 2018

> *I've learnt you are never too small to make a difference. And if a few children can get headlines all over the world just by not going to school, then imagine what we could all do together if we really wanted to.*

She asked the world to listen to climate scientists, who are warning that we're facing a climate emergency.

But what exactly does the science say?

11

The science of climate change

One of the longest weather records in the world is for central England. People have been recording temperatures here for almost 400 years! Scientists have compared this data and seen that the average temperature in central England over the last ten years was about 1°C warmer than it was 200 years ago.

Today, technology allows scientists to monitor every aspect of the climate.

A similar rise of 1°C has been measured around the world, and some places – such as the Arctic – are warming even faster than this. Although the average global temperature has naturally changed in the past, scientists believe it has never warmed this quickly before.

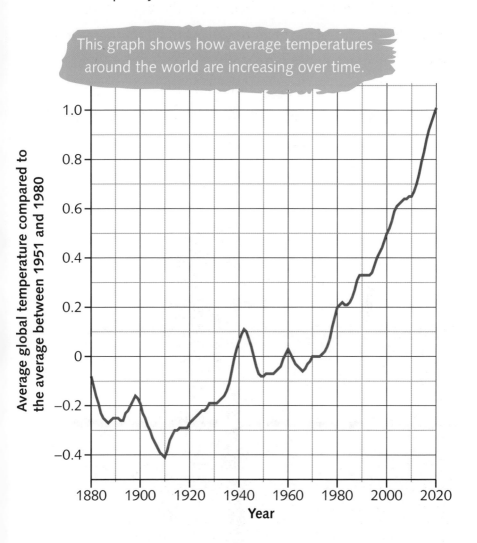

This graph shows how average temperatures around the world are increasing over time.

Some of the gases in Earth's **atmosphere** do the same job as the glass in a greenhouse. They let sunlight energy in, but trap some of this energy as heat so it doesn't all escape back into space.

the Sun

light energy from the Sun

Some heat energy escapes back into space, but some is trapped by Earth's atmosphere.

Some light energy is reflected by Earth's atmosphere and oceans.

Some of the Sun's energy is absorbed by Earth and released again as heat energy.

We need these **"greenhouse gases"**. Without them, Earth would be more like Mars, where the average temperature is minus 60° C – too cold for liquid water or for living things.

Mars

Venus

The planet Venus has far more greenhouse gases in its atmosphere than Earth does, which means it's a *lot* warmer – 460° C on average!

Why is the world getting warmer?

Around 200 years ago, the **Industrial Revolution** began, and the world changed in three ways:

1 People began burning large amounts of **fossil fuels** to heat and light homes, and to power transport and machines. This releases greenhouse gases into the atmosphere.

2 Forests were cleared to make way for farms, mines, roads and buildings. Trees soak up lots of greenhouse gases from the air.

3 Populations began to grow rapidly, which meant even bigger farms were needed to supply food. Farms release extra greenhouse gases.

Earth's atmosphere today contains far more greenhouse gases than it did 200 years ago, trapping more of the Sun's energy, so our planet is heating up. This is known as global warming.

In the early 1800s, about one billion people lived on Earth. Today it's 7.6 billion.

Why does global warming matter?

A temperature increase of 1 or 2°C doesn't sound too bad, but as the world gets warmer, scientists have noticed that the climate in different places is changing too.

Australia

rainforest

Some places, such as southern Australia, have a mild and wet climate. This is very different to the climate in a rainforest (hot and wet) or the Arctic (cool and dry). The climate in each place determines which plants can grow there, and which animals can live there. It affects how and where people live, and what kinds of farming they can do.

the Arctic

How is the climate changing?

In some areas of the world, such as Northern Europe and the Philippines, global warming is causing wetter weather and more floods. In other areas, such as California, USA, Australia and Afghanistan, extreme weather events, such as droughts, heatwaves and wildfires, are becoming more common.

Warmer temperatures also mean that glaciers and ice sheets are melting, and the average **sea level** has risen by almost 20 centimetres in the last 100 years.

These changes disrupt the delicate balance of life in each area, putting people, plants and animals at risk.

An evacuation centre for people displaced by severe flooding in the Philippines, 2018. The United Nations predicts that millions of people will be forced to move region or even country due to climate change.

Climate scientists use computer programs to help predict what Earth's climate will be like in the future. They've discovered that if we keep releasing extra greenhouse gases into the atmosphere, global warming will continue. The effects of climate change will get worse, for humans and for wildlife.

Some animals, such as corals, are very sensitive to changes in temperature. If the world warms by 2°C, scientists predict 99% of corals will die, and the thousands of species that depend on coral reefs will be lost too.

The message is simple: we must reduce the amount of extra greenhouse gases in the atmosphere by:

1 releasing fewer greenhouse gases, for example, by burning less fossil fuel

2 soaking up some greenhouse gases from the atmosphere, for example, by planting more trees.

Coral bleaching caused by a rise in temperature.

The climate strike goes global

In 2016, almost every country in the world signed an action plan known as the "Paris Agreement", agreeing to reduce greenhouse gas **emissions** in order to try to limit global warming to 1.5°C above the average global temperature before the Industrial Revolution.

Even with 1.5°C warming, the world faces big changes.

sea level rises 48 cm by 2100

increased flood risk

fewer fish in the oceans

more coral reefs lost

24

However, by 2018, the world's leading climate scientists warned that change wasn't happening quickly enough.

The climate strikers felt angry about this. Why weren't governments acting as quickly as they would in any other emergency?

severe droughts and heatwaves

smaller habitats for many plants and animals

lower crop yields

By March 2019, more than two million students in 135 countries had taken part in school strikes and events raising awareness about the climate crisis.

In May 2019, the UK became the first country to officially declare that it is facing an environment and climate emergency. Since then more than 15 other countries have done the same.

Adults began joining in too. People in positions of power started to notice – and to act. Governments around the world began to officially recognise the climate emergency, promising to put climate change at the centre of their decision-making.

At the start of August 2019, over 400 young climate activists from 38 countries gathered in Switzerland to discuss their campaign. They wrote this **manifesto**:

✓ **1** Keep the global temperature rise below 1.5° C.

✓ **2** Ensure climate justice.

✓ **3** Listen to the best united science.

Climate justice means that everyone takes a fair share of the action needed against climate change. Rich households and countries, who have more and use more, should make bigger changes than poorer households and countries.

This manifesto led to the biggest ever climate protests in September 2019. More than 13 million people participated in 7500 cities around the world, sounding the alarm louder than ever before.

'll TAKE MY EXAMS WHEN YOU KE ACTION

IF PEO ON U STRA

IF CL WA IT U BE E

ITS GETTIN HOT IN HERE

What can I do?

The school climate strikes are just one way in which young people can speak up and take action for the climate. There are lots of other ways to make an impact – many without even leaving your home!

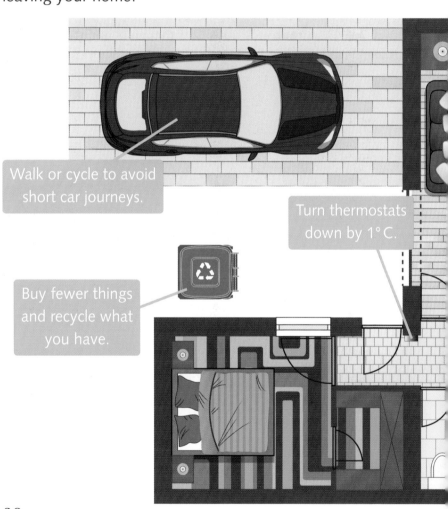

Walk or cycle to avoid short car journeys.

Turn thermostats down by 1°C.

Buy fewer things and recycle what you have.

Most homes rely on fossil fuels for lighting and heating. Fossil fuels might be burnt in your home directly (such as in a gas boiler) or may be used far from your home (such as at a power station that burns coal).

Switch off lights in empty rooms.

Block any draughts.

Eat less meat.

Take shorter showers.

Think local

Climate change isn't just happening in faraway places like the Arctic. Look out for local campaigns you can support or get involved in, from planting new trees to forming a school eco club.

Help wildlife

The United Nations has predicted that a million types of animals may become extinct due to climate change. This includes hundreds of species that live near you. You can help local wildlife by rewilding a garden or part of your school grounds, allowing grass and weeds to grow and letting nature take care of itself.

Spread the word

Even if you're not old enough to vote or make the rules, you are never too young to speak up and influence people who do have power – from parents/carers to politicians.

Greta Thunberg believes that most people would try much harder to tackle the climate emergency if they knew more about it. Encourage people to act by talking to them about the climate emergency.

You could try:

✓ writing to your local councillor or Member of Parliament about your climate concerns

✓ writing a story, making art or holding a cake sale to tell others about climate science in a creative way

✓ asking a parent/carer to make changes to the way they live

✓ organising a swapping event with friends – swap clothes, books, games or gadgets, so you buy less stuff.

Knowledge is power

Knowledge is important in the fight against climate change. Many young activists first learn about environmental issues by watching nature films and documentaries. Here are some suggested books and documentaries you can look up. You can have a look in your local library to see what you can find on this topic.

What Happened When We All Stopped
by Tom and Bee Rivett-Carnac

Greta's Story: The Schoolgirl Who Went on Strike to Save the Planet
by Valentina Camerini, Moreno Giovannoni and Veronica Carratello

This Book Will (Help) Cool the Climate
by Isabel Thomas and Alex Paterson

There Is No Planet B
by Mike Berners-Lee

No One is Too Small to Make a Difference
by Greta Thunberg

You can also search for these websites online:

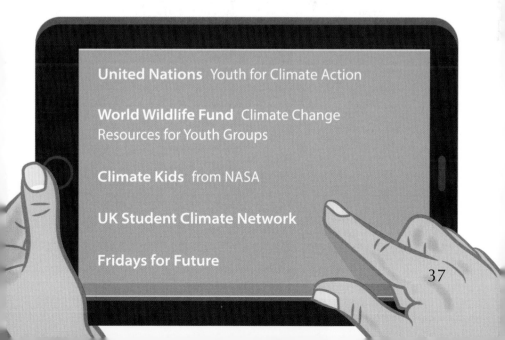

United Nations Youth for Climate Action

World Wildlife Fund Climate Change Resources for Youth Groups

Climate Kids from NASA

UK Student Climate Network

Fridays for Future

What next?

By the end of 2019, the climate strikers were making sure that climate change was headline news around the world. More than 1500 authorities in 30 countries had officially recognised the climate emergency.

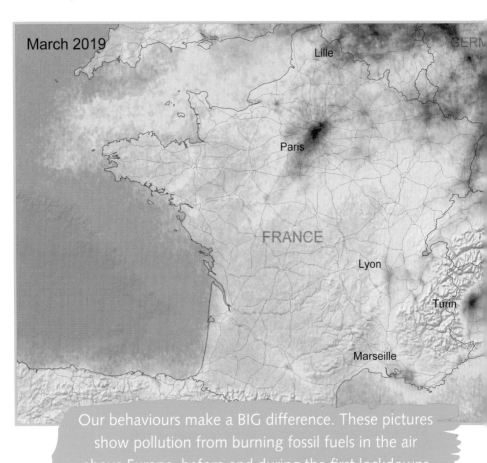

March 2019

Lille

GERM

Paris

FRANCE

Lyon

Turin

Marseille

Our behaviours make a BIG difference. These pictures show pollution from burning fossil fuels in the air above Europe, before and during the first lockdowns to stop the spread of COVID-19.

Then the world was hit by another crisis – a new type of coronavirus that caused a disease known as COVID-19. Many countries tried to stop COVID-19 spreading by asking people to stay at home as much as possible. Important meetings to discuss the climate emergency were postponed, including the 26th UN Climate Change Conference. Climate strikes were paused too.

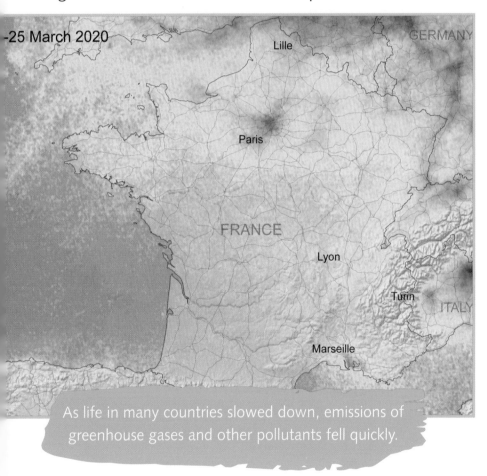

25 March 2020

Lille

GERMANY

Paris

FRANCE

Lyon

Turin

ITALY

Marseille

As life in many countries slowed down, emissions of greenhouse gases and other pollutants fell quickly.

The coronavirus crisis and the climate emergency have some things in common. There are no easy answers or quick solutions. Both can only be tackled if countries plan carefully and act together. Both require leaders to look carefully at the science and take the right decisions at the right time.

Both crises also show how the actions of normal people can add up to make a big difference.

The coronavirus crisis raised lots of questions about the future of the planet. Would we return to normal once the virus was under control, or try to do things differently? Could a less busy and polluted world be healthier for people as well as the planet?

A new chapter

The school climate strikes are just the beginning. The story of climate change is still being written – and you get to help decide how it ends.

Millions of young people who took part in the climate movement will soon be old enough to vote – and become scientists, politicians and business people themselves. Soon you and your friends will be the ones making decisions that affect the planet.

Climate strikers understand that we've all helped to cause the problems of climate change, so we all share responsibility for tackling them.

What can you do to help make our planet a cleaner, fairer, healthier place to live?

Glossary

atmosphere the blanket of air surrounding Earth. Air is
a mixture of different gases.

climate a typical pattern of weather in one place throughout
the year

climate emergency a term used to describe climate
change, which recognises that the world needs to take
action urgently

emissions greenhouse gases released into the atmosphere

fossil fuels fuels formed from plants and animals over
millions of years, such as coal, oil or natural gas

general election when people in a state or country vote for
representatives who will make up the government

greenhouse gases gases in Earth's atmosphere that trap heat
and warm Earth's surface

Industrial Revolution a period of very fast changes in
technology, farming and the way people lived in certain
parts of the world

manifesto a declaration of aims or actions that a group is
planning to take

sea level the level of the world's oceans compared to the land

What can you do?

LISTEN TO CLIMATE SCIENTISTS

DEMAND THAT ADULTS TACKLE THE CLIMATE EMERGENCY

RAISE AWARENESS

MAKE YOUR VOICE HEARD

PROTECT LOCAL ANIMAL HABITATS

PLANT MORE TREES

FIND WAYS TO BURN LESS FOSSIL FUEL

WALK OR CYCLE WHEN YOU CAN

TURN THERMOSTATS DOWN

WRITE TO PEOPLE IN POWER

TAKE RESPONSIBILITY

BUY FEWER THINGS

 Ideas for reading

Written by Gill Matthews
Primary Literacy Consultant

Reading objectives:

- Check that text makes sense, discuss understanding and explain meanings of words in context
- Identify main ideas drawn from more than one paragraph and summarise these
- Retrieve and record information from non-fiction

Spoken language objectives:

- Articulate and justify answers, arguments and opinions
- Give well-structured descriptions, explanations and narratives for different purposes, including for expressing feelings
- Participate in discussions, presentations, performances, role play, improvisations and debates

Curriculum links: Geography – Human and physical geography; Science – Living things and their habitats; States of matter

Interest words: climate strikes, climate change, climate movement, climate strikers

Build a context for reading

- Show children the front cover of the book. Ask what they think the title might mean. Link the word *strike* to the photo and ensure children understand what a strike is.
- Read the back cover blurb. Explore children's existing knowledge of the school strikes and who they think the one teenager might be.
- Establish that this is an information book. Ask children what features are usually found in non-fiction books.
- Turn to the contents page and ask children to identify how the information is organised.

Understand and apply reading strategies

- Read pp2–3 aloud to the children, including some of the posters. Briefly summarise the main points given on these pages.